Dee

Jamaican Patois Dictionary

Revised Edition

Austin Macauley Publishers
LONDON * CAMBRIDGE * NEW YORK * SHARJAH

Copyright © Deeta S. Johnson 2025

The right of Deeta S. Johnson to be identified as author of this work has been asserted by the author in accordance with sections 77 and 78 of the Copyright, Designs and Patents Act 1988.

All rights reserved. No part of this publication may be reproduced, stored in a retrieval system, or transmitted in any form or by any means, electronic, mechanical, photocopying, recording, or otherwise, without the prior permission of the publishers.

Any person who commits any unauthorised act in relation to this publication may be liable to criminal prosecution and civil claims for damages.

A CIP catalogue record for this title is available from the British Library.

ISBN 9781035817696 (Paperback)
ISBN 9781035817702 (Hardback)
ISBN 9781035817719 (ePub e-book)

www.austinmacauley.com

First Published 2025
Austin Macauley Publishers Ltd®
1 Canada Square
Canary Wharf
London
E14 5AA

Special thanks to my youngest daughter Sonji Mitchell for helping to design the book cover. My daughter Jessie Moyo James and brother NAL Amos Johnson for their contributions to dabbling in Jamaican patios.

History

The island of Jamaica is thought to have been uninhabited until the Arawak Indians arrived from the mainland of America, about ten centuries before the earlier Spanish settlers.

The Arawak named the island XAYMACA, meaning 'land of wood and water'.

The Arawak population declined when the Spanish settlers moved in. Negro slaves were imported from Africa to cultivate the island for the first time in the fifteen century. The capital or new township, Spanish town, was established in what is now St Catherine in the county of Middlesex.

In the sixteenth century, the British captured the island from the Spanish. Most of the Spaniards were expelled from the island and made their way to Cuba and other places. Some fled to the hills and formed a settlement.

Jamaica was now under British rule. More slaves were brought in to grow crops such as sugar cane, coffee, tobacco and cocoa. Some African slaves rebelled against the British and joined the settlers in the hills. The descendants of these settlers exist in these areas to this day.

The capital was moved to Kingston in 1872.

English is the official language. A dialect known as patois, spoken by the indigenous people, is presented in this book.

The majority of the population belong to the Christian denomination.

The judicial system in Jamaica is based on British law.

Profile

Jamaica is an island in the Caribbean Sea. The closest Caribbean islands to Jamaica are Haiti to the east and Cuba to the north. And further from the north of Cuba, it is also close to Florida in the southern states of America.

Jamaica is a well-established tourist attraction with beautiful white sandy beaches. The temperature ranges from 29º–33º degrees all year around.

Jamaica has a rich tapestry of people and entertainment, and flora and fauna.

It is popular with tourists worldwide, especially Americans, due to its close proximity.

Jamaica has two international Airports. One at either end of the island, namely Kingston and Montego Bay.

The currency is the Jamaican Dollar divided into 100 cents.

Preface

Jamaican patois are extensively used in Jamaica and Jamaican communities around the world. It is spoken with a distinct accent and used especially when singing reggae and dancehall songs.

Jamaica is an English-speaking country, but a large percentage of the indigenous people choose to speak the Jamaican patios.

If the Jamaican patois is spoken in a television documentary or drama, it is broad enough to warrant subtitles.

The language consists of words taken from other languages over the centuries and it had its origins in a time when the Jamaican economy was based on slavery.

The language comprises English, Spanish, African, Dutch, Creole, and Portuguese words that have been skilfully coined and devised by the native Jamaican.

Jamaica was first inhabited by the Arawak Indians, a migrating race of people from South America. Jamaica was later discovered by Columbus in 1494 and was named 'Jamaica' when he discovered the Americas.

After the Spanish rule, the island was ruled by the British for over 300 years and gained independence in August 1962. Jamaicans are a mixture of different nationalities since 1494 with surnames (and place names) originating from England, Scotland, Ireland, Spain, France, Africa, Portugal and Holland in fact, names encompassing all five inhabited continents of the globe.

The Jamaican patois is used in books, newspapers and advertising and on radio programmes in Jamaica.

My first impression on overhearing the patois was that it sounded light-hearted i.e. it is fruity, fun and airy and it rolls over the tongue easily. It can even sound romantic – romantic because it is created by the people. Whether spoken or sung, it can be used to express joy, gaiety, anger, seriousness, frivolity and simplicity. The old words have been handed down from generation to generation, and thousands of new words are being formed by present-day Jamaicans. Poets, singers, thespians and other wordsmiths find the language quite funny to play with.

It is not a recent language but is still evolving so there is a growing trend to preserve the Jamaican patois.

Climate

The climate is tropical. There is very little change during the seasons. The hottest months in Jamaica are June to September. The temperature is cooler in the hills and the mountains at night with the sea breeze in the day.

The rainy season is from October to November. There are many rivers in Jamaica, with waterfalls and rapids. Some rivers disappear underground through limestones and reappear again as mineral springs. The mineral springs are famous as spa baths among tourists.

Religion

The majority of the population belong to the Christian denominations. There are churches everywhere, e.g. Baptist, Methodist, Anglican, Pentecost Roman Catholic, Seventh-day Adventist, the church of God of Prophecy and Spiritualists i.e. revival cult e.g. "Pocomania" relating to the slavery of Africans.

The "Rastafarian", a widely known sect, founded in Jamaica is recognised as a religion. Its members are encouraged to return to Africa to settle through music, Reggae, poetry, authentic Rasta music with drums and chanting, and wearing of African tribal costumes.

Economy

The economy relies mainly on agriculture and tourism. Tourism is the second largest industry which provides work for the people incorporating e.g.:

Day Trips. Sight-seeing attractions.
Hotels. Beach tours.
Historical tours.
Great house tours.
Restaurant visits.
Horseback riding.
Rafting on the river.
Nature tours e.g. The Blue Mountains.
Waterfalls tours e.g. Dunn's River Falls.
Wild life tours e.g. Caves, bats, and crocodiles.
Water sports, i.e. sailing, skiing, swimming.

A – Z Patios Dictionary

A

Animul	Animal
Awhoo!	Who is it?
A who dat?	Who are you? Who is there?
Aise	Ear/Ears
A fi yuh	It is yours
A fi me	It is mine
A dem	It is them
A wha do yuh?	What is wrong with you?
A nuh nutten	It is nothing
Aenon town	Village near Norwood, Saint Ann
Appi	Happy
African flag Colours	Red, gold and green

Annatto/natto (The plant/seed) Used to colour soups, gravy, flour

B

Blue draws	See "tie-a-leaf"
Bumbo claat	Swear word, illegal in public
Backside	Bottom, bum, (exclamation word) *(What the Backside wrong wid yuh?)*
Big Bout yah	He/she is well known *(I'm popular!)*
Bruk	Broke down i.e. Car etc. *(De Fence pap dung)*
Bruk up	Party/dance etc. *(School bruk up or De fight bruk up)*
Befo day	Before sunrise, dawn, e.g. 4 a.m.
Bickle	Cooked food/a meal at home or restaurant
Batty hole	Swear word
Badmind	Covetous, jealous
Boasie	Flamboyant-proud
Butta pan	Empty butter pan
Black pan	Butter pan used for cooking
Backfoot	Exclamation word
Bam	Expression during conversation
Bax	To smack the cheeks

Blar	To brag
Backsiding	To chastise, beat physically
Bright	A confident, clever, intelligent child
Baal	To cry loudly
Bade	To bathe in the sea/river etc.
Babylon	A great empire/ruler of other nations(authority) (the police)
Beibi madda	A baby's mother
Backside	Exclamation word
Badwad	A swear word
Brushwood	Day sticks/wood for a campfire
Boadhouse	House made from wood, a hut
Backslide	One who stopped going to the church
Blasted	Mild swear word
Bantan	To ridicule
Bluebeat	Blues/rhythm/music
Bully beef	Corn beef
Bex	Vex
Bawn yah	This is my birthplace
Beible	Bible
Bun	See "Jacket" i.e. Bun in the oven

Busta	Treacle-type boiled sweet
Bwile	To cook, boil food etc.
Boonononous	Voluptuous woman
Baptise	Immersed underwater by the priest
Bread back	Crust, toppers (UK regional)
Bird pepper	Chilli peppers
Banana-green	Staple food, boiled with other starchy foods i.e. yam and potatoes
Bag juice	Crushed ice with syrup in a bag
Bruk-dung	Break down, i.e. appliance etc.
Bruk-up	Break up, i.e. relationships etc.
Bacci	Tobacco
Boopsie	An attractive obese woman
Backwud	Low intelligence
Babbicue	Balcony
Backfoot	Surprise. Expression
Backside	Mild swear word
Bulb	Protruding eyes (comical)
Bellyful	Satiated, not hungry
Browning	Girl with light brown/olive skin
Banana pap	Porridge made with green bananas
Babylon	Large colonial countries e.g. UK/USA

Backayard	Birthplace, homeland
Bailey	Small village near Norwood ST Ann, high ground
Bammy	Flat cassava bread to be fried before eating
Beibi	Baby
Backbiter	Angry person, quarrelsome
Breadfruit	A staple food for boiling or roasting
Bath pan	Large aluminium pan used for bathing
Bad boy	Lawbreaker, antisocial
Badman	Lawbreaker
Bud	Birds
Bruckfus	Breakfast
Backslide	Non-Christian. Stop going to church
Battyole	The anus, swear word
Bizzey	Tea herbal antidote for poison e.g. Slow poison or food poison
Bright	Intelligent. A cheeky, precocious child. *(yuh tuh bright)*
Bush doctor	Obeah man, witchdoctor
Belly battam	Abdomen
Belly button	Navel

Bettanh	i.e. better than

C

Crab toe	Unkempt toenails
Cooler	Prison
Claat	Cloth material, swear word
Cock-up	A plan gone wrong
Chatterbox	Mobile phone, cell phone
Coocumba	Cucumber
Cornmeal pap	Cornmeal porridge
Cocoa bea	Chocolate
Cocoa	Root vegetable
Cocoa tea	Mild chocolate with milk (Hot)
Chalklit tea	Hot chocolate with milk (Richer)
Chalklit	Chocolate powder
Coule	Cold temperature/body or air
Cole	Wood burning coal
Clath	Dress material
Cya	Cannot
Cyarry	Carry
Cyatch	Catch a train etc.
Chow ziz	Trouser, long pants
Chatty-chatty	Animated, lively, talkative

Crocodile wata	Unemotional tears
Corporation pop	Tap water
Cyaan	Cannot
Cus	Swear, argue
Cane piece	Sugar cane plantation
Seenoh	Snow, winter white flakes
Craw	Throat
Cigarette	Felt tip white stick with ginger hair
Cave valley	Village near Norwood, a cattle market
Cammilan	Village near Cave Valley
Coco piece	Shortcut leading to Cave Valley
Cut-up	Vex
Cane juice	Sugar cane juice/extract
Chemise	Long vest
Caramba	Expression/Surprise
Cut an swalla	Eating without chewing quickly
Creator	God of all things
Coronation market	Popular market near downtown Kingston. Farmers travel there from rural Jamaica to sell their produce

Criss	Smart, attractive
Cool	Smart, clever, easy
Callie	Type of ganja
Chillum	Ganja pipe, religious
Crabbit	Angry, aggressive
Chatterbox	Mobile/cell phone
Culcha	A cultured, educated person
Cassava dumpling	Made with cassava flour
Croaken	Lizard, gecko
Concrete jungle	City town/crowd
Coolie	African/Indian offspring
Cock-up	Mess up plans
Clappaz	Christmas crackers/fireworks
Caan meal pap	Corn meal porridge
Crawby	Old, infirm person, slow
Chuze	Choose
Cassava	Root vegetables, made into flour
Chimmy	Chamber pot, potty
Cave valley	St Ann neighbourhood hamlet that serves as a cattle market
Cane	Sugar cane plants are grown abundantly to produce rum, sugar, molasses

Crabbit	Jamaican Scottish word (Similar meaning)
Coconut	Tropical fruit of the coco palm tree versatile in cooking
Calypso	Steel pan Caribbean music invented in Trinidad sometimes skilfully played to the beat of reggae
Corporation pop	Pipe/tap water

D

Douse	Those
Daub	Smear, smudge
Degeh-degeh	Only one (to emphasise)
Dark/dawk	Not enlightened
Diss	Disrespect
Drop wud	To criticise within earshot
Dry yeye	Bare face
Dem nuh	They are not
Dunce	Illiterate, cannot read or write
Don	Boss, manager of a group/firm
Drumpan	Oil drum used to store rainwater
Dryland tourist	Dressed-up local person

Duckonoo	See "tie a leaf"
Dry malice	To ignore someone
Dut	Earth, dirt, ground
Duppy conqueror	Brave, fearless, not afraid of humans or ghosts
Dancehall music	Special genre of music, i.e. Dancehall Queen etc.
Dryhead	Short, unconditioned hair
Dub	Heavy bass/rhythm
Dasheen	Staple food/root vegetable
Dancehall queen	Crowned female/best dancer
Dancehall Artist/singer/songwriter/performer	
Dancehall DJ/selector/selecta	
Dese	These
Dance moves e.g.	Calypso, Reggae, Rub-a-dub, Rocksteady, Ska, Skank
Drug store	Pharmacy, chemist
Duckanse	Red ants
Doctor bud	Tiny bird. National bird
Dashwey	Throw away
Dalli-ouse	Girls' doll's house
Disrespek	No respect for someone

Dash	To throw
Drawdung	To lose weight i.e. someone
Draps	Cake made with diced coconut and sugar
Dead ouse	Funeral parlour
Duppymeka	A prolific gunman
Dress length	Material sold to dressmakers for a dress e.g. 3 yds.
Dunn's Riva	One of the eight rivers in Ocho Rios leading to the sea
Dour	i.e. door
Drah	i.e. draw (*Nuh drah mi tung*)
Dunn's River Falls	World-famous waterfalls, near Ocho Rios, visited by locals and tourists-supervised to climb and descend by guides

E

Evnin	Evening
Etna	Small oil stove to cook on
Eediat	Idiot, silly person
Eet	To eat fruits, snacks
Eggplant	Aubergine

F

Festival	Fried pancake, made with flour and sugar
Foce ripe	Unable to ripen, young fruit
Feel bad	Unwell, nauseous, bilious
Fresh	Catch a shower, freshen up
Fire wata	Rum, overproof, alcohol
Firetick	Outdoor wood for making fire
Foreign	Overseas land, e.g. USA etc.
Flour dumpling	Boiled dumplings (Dinner menu)
Flat bridge	A simple flat bridge built over Rio Cobre near Spanish town
Faas	Inquisitive, nosey
Flashlight	Torch
Fallah fashin	Copycat
Floor show	Cabaret, tourist/hotel entertainment
Fling wey	Throw away
Fatty bum bum	Obese women/Song record
Fleuraz	Flowers/flowas
Fishy	Vagina of a young girl
Fling weh	Throw away
Fits	Epilepsy, convulsion
Fahwud	Cheeky, feisty, precocious

Firecrackers	Fireworks, bangers
Flag	Banner
Firefly	Insect: i.e. Peenie Wallie "Firefly" house. Tourist attraction, burial place of English actor
Fern gully	Famous beauty spot near Milford/Ocho Rios. Drive-in through abundant ferns. HRH, The Queen travelled through there in 1953
Feel bad	To feel ill, faint or queasy
Food/menu	See page-
Fish tea	Thin broth made with fish, spring onions, cho cho + seasoning (hot) e.g. Salt + pepper
Food/menu Jamaican Bickle	Experienced worldwide A speciality remembered for its taste, meats marinated overnight
Foce-up	Someone too friendly, but company not welcomed (see p32)add this to it

G

Green/odour	The smell of body odour, sweaty
Git up	Get up
Gaad	Jehovah God
Guinep	Kind of plum, like lychees
Ground dove	Wood pigeon
Ghetto paradise	The sea-side resort, informal song
Gangan	Baby's grandmother
Guava	Small fruit used for jam/jelly
Grudgeful	Jealous, envious
Gran maakit	Christmas Eve market
Green	Naive, inexperienced
Grung	Allotment, small farm
Gungo peas	Small peas, used with rice or stew
Ghetto blaster	Large portable radio
Gutside (Mother's word)	Ribs (informal)
Gladys	Easily excited, i.e., women
Garden egg	Aubergine/eggplant.
Gun eena baggy	Female with venereal disease. V.D
Gleaner	National newspapers, sold worldwide to the diaspora.

	Discovered in the early 18th century
Green lizard	Tree lizard that changes its colour from brown to green to match its mood
Galling	Thin bird, e.g. The crane or a name for a tall scrawny girl

H

Heat	To reheat food
Har	Her
Heet	Raised temperature, body or air
Hampa	Wicker basket
Him	Him, he
Hole an/heng an	Hold on, hold tight, stop
Han	Hand
Hancart	Hand cart
Hardaise	Stubborn, play deaf
Hopscotch	Child's game
Haaba shark	A greedy person
Hard up	Broke, penniless, no money
Hominy	Crushed corn/maize

Head-tie	Scarf worn on the head
Haile Selassie	Revered by Rasta Farians
Howdie	Hello
Hail!	Greetings, i.e. Rasta style
Hell (What the) He 2 stick	Hell (comical)
Hanmiggle	Hand centre area, palm
Halla	Cry loudly, bawl, wail
Higler	Market/street trader
Hummingbird/doctor bud	Swallow-tail, hummingbird. Flies backward or hovers
Haile se lassie	Ethiopian king. Rasta Farians God Head (RETURNED CHRIST)
Hummingbird	Jamaica's "National Bird" has unique iridescent/blue/green colours indigenous to Jamaica
Hanback	Back of the hand, opposite of the palm
Hout	Out(*De fyah gone hout*) Patios
He 2 stick	Hell(comical)

I

I and I	Rasta saying: I/me, only one
Ilan boy	Jamaican boy, born and bred
Ilan girl	Jamaican girl, born and bred
Irish moss and linseed punch	Drink made from sea-weed, linseed and stout
Irish moss	Dried seaweed (edible)

J

Jackfruit	Large-segmented, sweet, fibrous fruit
Jamming	Disco dancing
Jeezas	Jesus or Christ
Jinx	Bad luck
Jeezam piece	Expression
Jerk chicken	Chicken barbecued with jerk seasoning
Jerk pork	Pork with jerk seasoning
Jerk seasoning	Specialised all spice ingredients which marinate some meats
Jerry curl	Curly hairstyle
Jrinks	Drinks, fizzy pop or ice-cold
Juice	Fruit juice, e.g. orange etc.

Juicy	Ripe sweet fruit, e.g. mango
Jamrock	The island of Jamaica
Jacks	Dice to play a game
Jamaican National flag	Black, gold and green
Jehovah	The lord or God
Jackass	Male donkey
Jamaican proverbs/adages	Sayings etc.
Jah rasta Fari	Words chanted after singing a song. A speech, music or exaltation after religious worship. To the most high
Jamaican Bickle/food	See menu

K

Kinteet	Broad/grin exposing the teeth
Key card	The ace to win the game
Kinout	Something inside out
Knock knee	Arthritic or disabled
Kekeh	Exclamation word
Key soap	Hard bar soap to wash clothes

Koolo koolo	Plentiful, e.g. food, feast
Kaliss	Careless
Kool-aid	Iced soft drink
Kerchief	Handkerchief (Cloth)
Ketch	To catch something or someone

L

Lang	Long for/wish, long, tall
Leffi	Leave it alone/a thing
Leff	Left i.e. direction
Labba mouth	Very talkative, overt
Libatty	Impertinent, rude, insolent
Lick dung	To knock down, a person, house or thing
Langas	Friendly name for a tall man
Leggo beese	Wild, untamed animals
Lick	To hit someone physically
Lissn	Listen
Light	Lungs, i.e. organ
Lickey lickey	Greedy for anything
Lang talking	Boring, long speech
Lamp post	Street light
Lunch pan	Lunch box with handle

Lantan	Lantern, portable light
Line enn	Maternity hospital
Laas	Lost, e.g. money or thing
Lang yeye	Jealous, envious
Lunch pan	Lunch box, tin
Lauf	Laugh
Lettah/s	Letter/s

M

Mek wig goh	Let us go!
Me nah	I am not
Me mumma	My mother! (Exclamation word)
Mout	To banter, make friendly quips
Mento	Music with banjo guitar/flute
Merika	America/USA
Moon pon tick	Street light, lamppost
Mumma	Mother
Munks	Among
Mooma	Mumma
Madda	Female bush doctor
Monkey lotion	Acid used unlawfully
Miggle	Middle
Mingle	Mingle i.e. in a crowd

Mule	An infertile woman
Murder	To annihilate someone
Murderer	An assassin
Murderashan	Utter destruction, a calamity
Medicine man	Bush doctor
Mango bush/walk	Not cultivated/grows wild
Masquerade	Masked procession, Christmas
Mash up	Break up e.g. party or thing
Mint ball	Stripe mint sweets (popular)
Mongoose	Small (meerkat type) wild animal
Milford	Public school place in Ocho Rios (author's) origin
Mash-mash	Leftover (of anything) food, fruits, etc.
Mashmout	No teeth, no dentures
Mi gwine	I am going to, etc.
Mampi	Fat woman, strong and resourceful
Milford Riva	A small river near Milford School runs under a bridge

N

Necktie	Necktie, neckwear

Nose ole	Nostril/s
Nose naut	Secretion from nose
Nine nite	A wake, chanting nine nights after a funeral
Nashi	Nasty, dirty, unclean
Nylon road	Long smooth motorway
Needn	Need not
No badda	Don't worry
Nable tring	Navel, umbilicus cord
Nutten	Nothing
Nuff respek	A lot of respect
Nizey wata	The river mouth at Norwood used by villagers (to wash clothes) and fetch water

Number	
Wan	1
Too	2
Tree	3
Fore	4
Five	5
Sies	6
Seben	7
Ait	8

Nien	9
Ten	10
Illeben	11
Dozen	12
Terteen	13
Foteen	14
Fifteen	15
Siesteen	16
Sebenteen	17
Aiteen	18
Nineteen	19
Twenty	20
Terty	30
Fourtey	40
Fifty	50
Sistey	60
Sebenty	70
Aity	80
Ninety	90
Undred	100
Night nurse	Night carer
Nah	Name of Rasta man
Norwood	The author's birthplace

ST. Ann,
Jamaica W I

Neck side!	Exclamation word

O

Oil lamp	Kerosine/paraffin lamp
Oil machine	Car, van, truck etc.
Outa auda	Out of order
One love	Form of greeting, a famous song by Bob Marley
Oil skin	Floral patterned, plastic tablecloth
Ocho Rios Tourist Resort North Coast	Spanish for eight rivers/let flowing To the sea, e.g. Parry Town, Milford, Big River Shaw Park (Rain Forest) White River, culminating in Dunn's River (spectacular) Water Falls.

P

Punch	Eggnog, milk, stout, rum, nutmeg(Homemade)
Prangagnat	Pomegranate
Pineapple	Ananas comosus (Spanish)

Paradise plum	Red and white boiled sweet (fruit)
Pull up	Stop
Pom pom/pam pam	The sound of guns firing
Proppa	Proper
Press	To iron clothes
Pop style	To wear
Papdung	To collapse e.g. a fence
Proverb	Moral saying/meaning
Poopa/puppa	Father (Informal)
Paypa	Paper
Pitata	Potato
Peiple	People
Pear tree	Avocado tree (Central America) Aquacate tree (Spanish)
Pawn	To grab something or someone
Pap off	Break off
Parables	A saying related to the bible
Papaw	Papaya, a soft yellow fruit
Peg	A section of fruit, i.e. orange
Pantie	Knickers, women's underwear
Pot soup	Liquid drained after cooking vegetables (father's remedy!)

Punni punni	Weak, fragile person, sickly
Poco mania	Pocco religion
Pine	To fret, grieve
Pear	Jamaican pear, i.e. avocado
Poas	Fence post, a place to post a letter
Pudden	Cornmeal pudding/cake
	Sweet potato pudding
Pull up	Stop, hold on to the brakes
Prayer meeting	Early morning worship
Pickie pickie	Short dry unconditioned hair (fussy)
Pants length	Street vendor wares sold to men for tailoring
Patch	To repair a thing e.g. clothes, the roof
Puzzle	Riddle *(Riddle mi dis, riddle mi dat*
	One slice of white yam serves the whole world. (ansar) The Moon
	Riddle mi dis, riddle mi dat
	Who is a clever spider
	(ansar) bredda anansi)
Pun	*(Kekeh!*
	A who dat?
	A who dat?
	A who dat a say who dat
	When mia say who dat)

Q

Qeeze	Squeeze, to squeeze something
Query	To question something
Quashie	Someone not qualified to do an important job e.g. Doctor, teacher etc.

R

Rock stone	A stone, rock mountain or an exclamation word
Rudeboy	Behaving badly, anti-social
Rail up	Get angry quickly
Roadside	Grass verge
Rag	Face flannel etc.
Rasta fari	Greetings, chanting, exclamation word
Rock steady	Slow music, reggae 1960s
Riddim	Music to dance to the beat
Roots (authentic African culture)	Black culture, i.e. art, food, music, clothing, language, etc.
Roots reggae	Afro beat., Rasta farian reggae

Rio cobra	The river winding its way to the Caribbean Sea near Kingston Harbour
Rispek	Respect, a friendly greeting
Rub a dub	Rhythm bass
Run belly	Diarrhoea
Rasta music	Roots reggae with drums
Revival music	Religious music, e.g. pocomania with drums
Reader	Fortune teller
Raasing	To flog
Rastaurant	Caribbean café bistro/restaurant
Ruckshan	Quarrel, heated argument
Refreshment	Food and drink/snacks
Rum punch	See "punch"
Riva/s	Natural places of interest, i.e. beauty spots around the island, e.g. Milk River, Black River, Dunn's River and White River
Reilli	Really positive
Play tree	He/she is deceased
Roase	To roast meats/nuts etc.
Raas claat	Common swear word, illegal

Riddle	See "riddle, puzzle, conundrum"
Rundem	To chase away someone who is annoying

S

Shanty town	Underdeveloped/impoverish community
Skank	Dance hall, dance moves
Scotch bonnet	Garden pepper, very hot
Sleip	Sleep
Stush	Sexy looking attire
Suh	So
Salt	Broke skint
Slackness	Immoral, lewd
Stoshus	Proud
Ska	1960s pre-reggae music
Six foot six	Graveside measurement
Soun system	Jukebox/boxes
Stout	Port/wine for punch
Struwps	Hissing of teeth
Seetdeh	There it is
Sweet pitata	Sweet potato
Scandal bag	Black plastic/shopping bag

Showa/bathe	Shower or bath
Saul	Woman's vagina
Slow poison	Food poisoning etc.
Shuse	Shoes
Seenoh	Snow, sleet etc.
Skanking	Freestyle dance to reggae
Shuga an wata	Lemonade
Sky juice	Ice crushed with strawberry syrup in a bag
Shuga cane	Sugar cane, a plant
Sideman	Baggage handler on bus etc.
Shooter	A person with venereal disease
Shama macka	Mimosa shrubs shrink when touched
Swalla	To eat i.e. swallow
Singa	Singer/vocalist
Sedwey	No change in some way
Saaf	Soft, ripe, not hard(fruit)
Single bieble	Aloe vera treats the whole body e.g. skin, insect bites laxative, tonic, hair, sunburn, dry lips

Standpipe	Designated village stand-pipe for fetching clean water
Sarsaparilla	Look under
Spar	Friend, mate, buddy
Star	National newspaper
Seaside	Beach
Samefie man	Con man, scammer for money, witchdoctor
Sa'f	Soft
Saf jrinks	Soft drinks
Shublack	Hibiscus flower used to polish shoes
Skylark	To romp, play, carefree
Shutyeye	Sleep, long or short nap
Star!	Singer, respect/greeting
Spwile	Damaged e.g. food
Spwile sport	Serious, un-co-operative
Selecta	Record/CD selector, disc jockey
Standpipe	Communal water pipe for a village
Swibel up	To shrink
Seed	Kernel e.g. mango, avocado

Seed	Male testicle
Sinkhole	Crater caused by sudden depression of the earth
Sattiday	Saturday
Shawt	Short
Shawty	Friendly name for short
Shuga	Sugar made from sugar cane
Sour sop	Fruit/pulp used to make punch
Sweet sop	Small fruit cherimoya (Spanish)
Strong bak	Bark from tree boiled to make tonic
Sacks	Socks
Shet	Shut the door, window
Suda	Pacifier, baby's dummy
Soun bwoy	Jukebox, DJ
Staum	Storm, hurricane
Scratch-scratch	Irritating skin rash
Sinsemilla	Seedless marijuana
Shit	Illegal drugs
Silver bangle	Handcuffs
Sidewalk	Pavement
Shet pan	Pan with lid

Slate	Framed slate used in primary school
Sorrel	Flowers used to make wine
Susumba	Pea produce used for cooking
Saltfish	Cured, salted cod (imported) used in a recipe for a staple diet e.g. cabbage/Callaloo the national favourite dish ackee + saltfish or on its own
Saltfish/flittas(flittaz)	Fried pancake made with flour, onion, tomato, thyme etc.
School slate	Primary school writing tool
Scram	Go away, move
Shub	To push someone e.g. out of the way *(Yuh fren shub pass mi)* patios

T

Tek set	To hassle someone
Tings	Things
Trim	Man's haircut to trim
Tripe	Intestines, cow's stomach etc.

Touches	Ill-tempered, sensitive
Tump	Thump sound, to hit with the fist
Tracing/trace	To disgrace someone, curse them
Tumbledung	Fall/fell down anything
Tie head	Women's headscarf
Truss	Trust/to buy something on the slate
Tenement yaad	House with many tenants
Titty	Breasts (informal) e.g. teat
Tool	Gun firearm
Tyad	Tired
Trickster	Con man/woman, swindler
Tune	Heartwarming dance/music
Tun cornmeal	Seasoned polenta with water/cook slowly
Thatch walk	Thoroughfare hamlet leading to Norwood
Tam	Beret flat cap, round without peak
Trench town	Famous shanty town district in Kingston. Bob Marley and other reggae artists grew up in the 1960s
Trash out	Settle an argument, debate, discuss, argue with each other

Tamarind	Tropical fruit tree, pulp of fruit to make a drink
Tally	To count produce/goods etc.
Tallyman	To value goods etc.
Tekwey	To take away/move something

U

Urricane	Hurricane season, violent storm
Urtquake	Violent shaking of the earth's surface
Undred	Number to aim for
Usling	Barter Street peddling
Ussel	Hustle, sell goods on a street
Urt (Earth)	Our planet/world
Underpants	Man's briefs, Y fronts boxers

V

Veteran DJ	Famous disc jockeys, dancehall stars
Veterans	Famous reggae singers
Vital/ital	Foods suitable for vegetarians and vegans, e.g. nuts, greens, fruits

W

Wire Waase	Girl with tiny waist
Willy	Boy/ Man's penis
Wata Wash	Washed unironed clothes
West Indian	Old term for Caribbean people in 1960's
Wash Out	Purgative e.g. Senna, Enema
Wus	Worse
Wata Hole	Spring. Used by people or animal
Warner	A clairvoyant. Male or Female
Wash Wey	Result of a flood house, car, etc.
Well	Manmade water hole. Very deep
Walk Good	Good bye/ God go with you!
Weed	Cannabis/ Marijuana/ Ganja
Watch Yah	Look at this
Wacka	Bush wacka. Garden strimmer
Wee Wee	To urinate, i.e. childs expression
Whine	See: Grine
Wussa	Worse than
Wuk	Work, Labour, Toil
Whac Waan	How are thing? Popular saying!

X

Xeggs up	Too Friendly
Xplain	Explain i.e. Simplify
Xtra	Show off, Extrovert
Xma	Eczema, skin rash
Xaymaca	Old Arawak name for Jamaica
Xample	Example

Y

Yessiday	Yesterday
Yasso	Here
Yaad	Yard
Y'eye Carna	Eye corner
Yain Hill	Mound of Earth, where yam us planted
Yam piece	Yam farm/ Allotment
Y'eye Glass	Spectacles
Yam Bank	see: Yam Hill
Yeye Wata	Tears to cry

Z

Zebedee	Biblical name mother gave to one of her son
Zinc	Sheets of Zinc used for roofing house
Zing	Playground/ Swing

Jamaican proverbs

Proverb	Honour thy mother and thy father.
	Love thy brothers and sisters.
	Love thy neighbour.
Proverb	Time longer than rope.
Meaning	Time will tell, good or bad.
Proverb	Silent river run deep.
Meaning	Don't trust anyone or anything.
Proverb	Kill two birds/bud with one stone.
Meaning	Save time and money, quick solution.
Proverb	God don't give you more than you can bear.
Meaning	Trust god have faith, pray.
Proverb	Jump outa frying pan into the fire.
Meaning	They are the same, they have the same effect.
Proverb	God nah sleip.
Meaning	God is not sleeping, he is watching us.
Proverb	Tan pan crooked, cut straight.

Meaning	Things will improve.
Proverb	Every mickle mek a muckle.
Meaning	Every little thing helps.
Proverb	Once a man twice a child.
Meaning	To need help in old age.
Proverb	Who laughs last, laughs best.
Meaning	I am the winner, I have the upper hand.
Proverb	Wha drop offa head drop pan shoulder.
Meaning	You or your children will benefit.
Proverb	Hog say the first water, wash in it.
Meaning	Don't miss the first opportunity.
Proverb	Wantie wantie caan get it havie, havie no want it.
Meaning	You want what you don't care about.
Proverb	Bad luck worse than witchcraft/obeah.
Meaning	Bad luck is more potent than witchcraft.
Proverb	Every hoe ad a tick a bush.
Meaning	There is someone to suite everybody.
Proverb	One cocoa, full basket.
Meaning	Every little thing helps.
Proverb	Chicken merry hawl deh near.
Meaning	Merry-making usually ends in tears. e.g (children)

Proverb	Peace an love.
Meaning	Greetings! God be with you!
Proverb	Who caan hear wi feel.
Meaning	Take my advice or you will be sorry.
Proverb	You tuh red yeye.
Meaning	You are too greedy/jealous.
Proverb	Once a man twice a child
Meaning	Adults usually revert to their childhood.
Proverb	Everyday bucket a goh well, one day de battom a goh drap out.
Meaning	Nothing stays the same.
Proverb	When frog say him nah ramp "beware"!
Meaning	What is a joke to you is serious business to him.
Proverb	Wha nuh ded nuh ashey weh.
Meaning	Where there is life there is hope.

Jamaican Sayings/Adages

Saying/Adages	Puss an dawg nuh hab de same luck.
Meaning	Everyone's luck is different.
Saying	Si me an come liv wid mi a two diffran ting.
Meaning	Looks are deceiving, you are not loving and kind.
Saying	Tedeh fi me tomarra fi yuh.
Meaning	My bad luck today your turn tomorrow.
Saying	Him a gi lauf fi peas soup.
Meaning	He/she is very happy.
Saying	Two cousin bwile sweet soup.
Meaning	Those two cousins are lovers.
Saying	Scornful dawg nyam dutty pudden.
Meaning	Someone too fussy sometimes eats unclean food.
Saying	Mi a look a wuk.

Meaning	I am looking for a job, have you any work/vacancy?
Saying	Yuh gwine live long.
Meaning	I was just thinking about you e.g. called your name.
Saying	Dash wey belly.
Meaning	To have an abortion.
Saying	Monkey know which tree Fe clime.
Meaning	The strong always pick on the weak.
Saying	Dem a chat me.
Meaning	They are criticising me behind my back.
Saying	Grease mi palm
Meaning	Can you spare a dollar? I am broke/skint.
Saying	Cool like coocoomba.
Meaning	Easy going, placid nature.
Saying	Moon pon tick.
Meaning	Street light, lamp post.
Saying	Watch yah nuh.
Meaning	Listen carefully, hear this!
Saying	Sometime caafe, sometime tea.
Meaning	Time for a change.
Saying	Drop tune gimme yah.

Meaning	Play de music i.e. the music is good!
Saying	Him hab mi eeva him craw.
Meaning	He/she is angry with me.
Saying	Wha sweet nanny goat wi run him belly.
Meaning	Nice things can harm or affect you.
Saying	Horse dead an cow fat.
Meaning	Too many confusing/complicated stories. E.g. information
Saying	Duppy no who fi frighten.
Meaning	The strong always pick on the weak.
Saying	If yoh no ketch harry you ketch him shuth.
Meaning	If you don't catch the father you will catch the son.
Saying	Yoh gwine fenneh.
Meaning	You will be sorry.
Saying	It holey-holey but ee clean.
Meaning	My clothes are ragged but they are not dirty.
Saying	A we run tings.
Meaning	We are in charge i.e. the boss/managers.

Saying	Nobaddy move, nobaddy get hurt!
Meaning	Reggae song/lyrics/by veteran reggae artist.
Saying	Mi no count yuh.
Meaning	You are not my friend.
Saying	Dem a bench an batty.
Meaning	They are close friends.
Saying	Is it because I'm black?
Meaning	Reggae song lyrics, by veteran reggae artist.
Saying	Deh wid, him/she deh wid.
Meaning	A relationship. They are lovers.
Saying	Ole fire tick easy fi ketch.
Meaning	They are in love again.
Saying	Good fren betaan pocket money.
Meaning	A friend is sometimes more useful than money.
Saying	Yuh live long.
Meaning	Mi jus call yuh name.
Saying	Give thanks an praise to the most high Jah Rastafari
Meaning	God is good.
Saying	Wash Belly

Meaning	To have an abortion.
Saying	Kick the bucket.
Meaning	He/she is dead.
Saying	Tun back.
Meaning	Change course, go back, reverse etc.

Jamaican
Popular Sayings/Adages

Saying	Live in hope and die in constant spring. (two areas in Kingston)
Meaning	You may not get what you wish for.
Saying	Him a play fool fe ketch wise.
Meaning	He is acting silly to outsmart you.
Saying	High seat kill Miss Thomas puss.
Meaning	Don't aim higher than you can reach.
Saying	Fat like Miss Thomas Puss.
Meaning	Comical compliments, you look well.
Saying	Yuh free paper bun
Meaning	Your holiday is finished.
Saying	Hell eena powda house.
Meaning	All hell broke loose, aggressive arguments.
Saying	Leggo de ooman.
Meaning	Leave her alone.
Saying	Me and she nuh deh.

Meaning	We are not lovers.
Saying	Heng pon nail.
Meaning	Someone who is shabbily dressed.
Saying	Bob anh weave.
Meaning	Indecisive can't make up one's mind.
Saying	Nyam anh gowhey.
Meaning	To dine with someone and leave immediately after.
Saying	Me anh him nuh tek tea.
Meaning	We don't like each other, we don't agree.
Saying	Blouse anh skirt!
Meaning	Comical expression.
Saying	Kiss me neck!
Meaning	Surprise remark/reply.
Saying	What a bam bam.
Meaning	What a carry-on, it's hilarious!
Saying	Kick the bucket/play three.
Meaning	He is deceased.
Saying	Me a goh a foreign.
Meaning	I am going overseas. USA, Canada, UK, etc.
Saying	Tek sleip mark death.
Meaning	They resemble each other. Be careful.

Saying	Rain a fall but dutty tuff.
Meaning	Things seem okay but it is not.
Saying	Nuh Badda wid de crocodile wata.
Meaning	Those are not real tears, you are pretending.
Saying	Stop beat up yuh gum.
Meaning	Shut up, stop nagging/arguing talking etc.
Saying	Yuh mussi mad.
Meaning	What you are saying is not true/nonsense.
Saying	Laud a massi dawg a fassi.
Meaning	Comical reply. I am surprised!
Saying	Pap torey gimme yah.
Meaning	Tell me more, elaborate.
Saying	Unoo tuh lickey lickey.
Meaning	You are all too greedy.
Saying	Hole dawg.
Meaning	Hold your dog before I enter.
Saying	A reddi mi reddi an a gone mi gone.
Meaning	I am leaving now.
Saying	Don't waste powder pon black bud.
Meaning	Don't waste time unnecessarily.
Saying	Tap beat up yuh gum.
Meaning	You talk too much!

Sayings + Adages + Proverbs

Saying	Look before yuh leap.
Meaning	Weigh things up before making a decision.
Saying	Who caan hear wi feel.
Meaning	If you don't listen to advice you will suffer somehow.
Saying	Belief kill an belief cure.
Meaning	Think carefully about what you believe in, think twice.
Saying	Time langa dan rope.
Meaning	Time will solve every problem.
Saying	Weepin an wailin.
Meaning	Loud, emotional crying.
Saying	Sum a dem a holla sum a baal.
Meaning	To cry loudly i.e. distraught.

Jamaican Proverbs

Proverb/saying	Don't dig one ole. Dig two.
Meaning	If you set a trap for someone set one for yourself also.
Saying	Nutten nuh goh so.
Meaning	It's a lie, none of it is true.
Saying	A who yuh a talk tuh.
Meaning	Stop disrespecting me.
Saying	Ole firetick easy fe ketch.
Meaning	Past lovers will easily be lovers again.
Saying	Him tek milk outa caafe.
Meaning	He is a professional thief.
Saying	Horse ded an cow fat?
Meaning	Too many useless stories! Something is not true.
Saying	If yuh waan good yuh nosehaffi run.
Meaning	You need to work hard to be successful.

Saying	Dutty wata good fi hout fire.
Meaning	Anything that can make peace, use it.
Saying	A nuh everything good fi talk.
Meaning	Keep some cards close to your chest.
Saying	When haus ded anh cow get fat.
Meaning	Some or some things benefit.
Saying	Cock mout kill cock.
Meaning	Idle talk/shoot oneself in the foot.
Saying	Empty bag caan tan up.
Meaning	A hungry man is a lazy, angry man.
Saying	Strike while de iron is hat.
Meaning	Don't pass up an opportunity.
Saying	Don't sorry fi maaga dawg.
Meaning	
Saying	Because! Maaga daws wi byte you.
Meaning	

N.B popular Jamaican sayings

- Doah trow weh you stick before yuh.
  Cross the bridge.
  Don't invite trouble.

- Nuh drah mi tongue.
  Do not let us argue or quarrel with each other.

- Wha drap offa head drap pon shoulda.
  What are loose, another one gain.

- Wen wan dour shut, One dda wan upun shut.

- Yuh lie? That is a surprise.
  A lie? I can't believe it!

- Dawg nyam yuh supper.
  Means you are in big trouble.

- Yuh name is mud.
  Everyone thinks you are rubbish.

- Yuh nuh cut nuh dash.
  You are not dressed/looking smart.

- Pipe dung.
  (you talk too much)
  Stop arguing.

- (Patois) Gimme pass (local lingo).
  Move out of the way.

- (Patois) Move wey deh (common lingo).
  Excuse me, please.

- (Patois) Mi deh yah (common lingo).
  I am in here.

Food-Menu-Fruits-Drinks

Bruckfus: Breakfast

1. Ackee + saltfish + boiled
   Green bananas or roast breadfruit

   Or

   Fried plantin' or fried dumpling

2. Porridge variety (PAP)
   Cornmeal
   Banana
   Hominy corn
   Rice

3. Liver or mutton

   +

   Boiled bananas (Green)

4. Saltfish + calaloo (salt Cod + spinach)

   +

Boiled green bananas (or) fried breadfruit

5. English Breakfast
   Eggs
   Toast
   Marmalade
   Jam
   Coffee, Tea, Tea infusions (Mint etc.)
   Bread + Butter supplement

6. Bammy/ fried cassava bread + ackee + saltfish

Lunch or Snack

Bun + cheese sandwich
Avocado pear slice/peg   side dish
Cold drink: desired

Sandwiches: ham, cheese
Side salad: lettuce, tomato, cucumber, avocado
Drink: hot or cold
Lager. Beer

Bammy + fried fish (fried bammy)
Drink: hot or cold

Fried dumplings + ackee + salt fish
Ripe plantin' (fried) (breakfast choice)
Drink: desired
Fried fish: whole or filleted + escovitch onions + peppers + tomato
Bread + butter + sweet potato sauteed

Drink: desired, hot, cold (or) alcoholic

Bulla cake + cheese
Bulla cake + avocado + butter
Salt fish fritters   (flittaz) Sandwich filler
Side salad: lettuce, tomato.

Fruit salad
Ice cream
Drink: hot, cold, lager/beer (desired)

Dinner Menu
Local (or) National

1) Saturday   5-6 P.M.

Beef stew   Soup or mutton casserole

Casserole   1–6 person

1 peg/slice of breadfruit

1 slice yellow yam

1 Irish potato – 1 white flour dumpling

Carrots, pumpkin + thyme.

Seasoning, i.e. spring onions, salt, chilli, pepper

2) Sundays   1-6 P.M.

Rice + peas. red peas/kidney beans

Fried chicken or jerk chicken

Vegetables, i.e. carrots, onions, garlic + gravy

Side salad, i.e. lettuce, tomato, cucumber

3) Monday – Thursday

Pork dinner fried or stewed

Steamed fish, i.e. sea bass, mullet, salmon, bream etc.

Plain rice i.e. White Rice

Root vegetable or green banana, yam etc.

Curried goat/beef/pork.

Ox tail stew with white rice salt fish + cabbage + White rice

4) Fridays

Seasoned corn beef + steamed rice or

Fried dumplings + ackee + salt fish or

Porridge + fried dumpling + fried ripe plantin' + Ackee + Salt fish

Soup variety overleaf

Soups Varieties Monday–Friday

Red peas soup

Gungo peas soup

Fish tea

Black-eyed peas soup

Pumpkin soup

Chicken soup

Pepper pot soup

Beef soup

Drinks Hot + Cold

Jrinks: Cold

Lemonade, ginger beer

Sorrel Lager, beer-punch (Alcoholic)

Ice water

Fruit juices e.g. orange juice, coconut water, pineapple juice.

Rum, whiskey, gin, cocktails, aperitifs

Soursop punch

Irish moss + linseed punch

Passion fruit punch

Carrot juice + stout

Red wine

White wine

Tia Maria, aperitif cocktail

Jrinks: Hot

Coffee

Tea

Chocolate (richer/sweeter)

Cocoa (milder)

Medicinal:

Ginger tea

Bush /green tea, guinea hen tea

Mint tea	Antacid
Fever grass tea	Fever
Tamarind leaf tea	Measles
Bissey tea	Antidote
Ceresse tea	Stomach ache
Sarsaparilla	Tonic

Fruits: Grown locally

Cherries

Bananas

Oranges

Grapes

Guinep

Jackfruit

June plum

Guavas
Star apple
Rose apples
Mangoes
Naseberry
Tangerine
Tamarind

Custard apple/sweet sop	(Cherimoya)-(Spanish)
Sour sop	Annona muricate
Pineapple	Ananas comosus

Types of mangoes (Mangifera indica)

Beefy	Round and large
Blackie	small/Green skin
Common	hog mangoes
East Indian	grows on a very low tree
Julie mangoes	kidney shape/Green skin
Stringy	Yellow/kidney shape
Sweetie mango	yellow skin
Turpentine	kidney shape/distinct taste

The Enlightenment

Martha Faraday, a widow, had two grown-up children who chose careers she neither knew nor cared about.

She made her livelihood from the little bakery her husband, Jake, had left her, without any help from her children, Pete or Connie.

Connie was always going off to wild locations to do her modelling. This worried Martha because Connie was once mauled by a wildcat in the African jungle, pecked by a vicious bird in the Caribbean, and carried away by an angry elephant she was riding in the Himalayas. As for Pete, Martha lost count of the many black eyes and bruises he collected during his boxing career.

Everyone close to her warned her about becoming a nervous wreck if she did not pay less attention to the bakery and get out more. In such a small village as theirs, Martha could not envisage herself adopting a new, more exciting lifestyle, even though she was only forty-four. But when Connie invited her on a holiday trip to watch her modelling work, little did she know that the journey was to change the humdrum routine she was used to into a life of glamour and excitement, which would make even her daughter jealous.

"Are you sure you want me to chaperone you to Jamaica?" she asked, thinking she had misheard.

"Certainly," Connie replied without hesitation. "Jamaica can be a pretty scary place at times still, you know."

"How scary do you mean?" asked an anxious-looking Martha. "You don't mean there are wild animals walking around the tents at night, do you?"

Connie scratched her head and continued to sort out her wardrobe. "Not exactly, Mother, but pretty close to it. It's possible they will have animals in cages or on leads to complement the setting."

Martha looked at her worriedly. "I'm not sure I want to be in the company of wild animals, Connie, cages or no cages. At the same time, I suppose I'd better be brave and go with the saying 'I'll try anything once'."

"That's the spirit," Connie replied, smiling. "We leave in a month's time, so have your wardrobe, your passport and your traveller's cheques ready by then. And by the way, Barney Miller has decided to pay half our return fare."

"That's very nice of him, but who is Barney Miller?"

"Oh, he's the boss of the agency that employs me. Since you are acting as chaperone, they figured they owe you a discount."

Martha looked at her, wide-eyed with curiosity. "I hope there are no chores involved. I'm going for a rest. Slaving over a hot oven all these years deserves a nice rest."

Connie gave her a quick look and a wry smile.

"You'll get plenty of rest, but I dare if you're standing around and doing nothing you'll be asked to serve beverages or hold an umbrella. That sort of thing will earn you some compliments. The natives love it."

"I can see what sort of holiday I'm going to have with you to look after," Martha replied, laughing.

A month later, five of them piled out of a hired wagon at the airport to board the plane. There was the chief photographer, Miles, his assistant, Roland, Debbie, a second model, and Connie. As they struggled through the airport barriers with their hand luggage, Martha could see a whole new world opening up in front of her. Until then she had never realised that so many people travelled the earth. People were going north, east, west and south for hundreds of different reasons.

As she watched a variety of humans helter-skeltering about, she stumbled over someone's suitcase before suddenly realising that her party was way ahead of her, going towards the runway.

Connie stepped out of line, waited for her and gave her an impatient look.

"Try and stick with the group, Mother, or we may lose each other."

Martha, fighting her way through the crowd, told her, "Never mind me, you go ahead and sit with your friends. I'll be on the plane."

Connie gave a bemused smile. "You won't be able to sit where you like, Mother, furthermore, our tickets are probably all consecutive."

Connie was wrong about the tickets. Martha had bought hers separately, and she had to sit elsewhere. This pleased Martha because she did not feel obliged to chat with the stranger sitting next to her; she therefore had plenty of time to muse.

As she sat looking out of the window at the white clouds and endless expense of ocean beneath her, she thought about the little bakery she had left behind. It was not closed, she had left her cousin, Walter to run it. She had felt sorry for Walter ever since he became almost paralysed and unfit for work. Having an emotionally weak-willed wife like Phyllis, and a young son at boarding school, did not help his position either.

Yes, she thought, *Walter will certainly amuse himself while I'm away.*

Several hostesses walked around, serving cocktails. Martha relaxed in her seat, sipped her rum 'bamboozle' and listened to the ebbing sound of drums and maracas in the background. Mesmerised by the whole affair, she dozed off, thinking she could not take it all in.

In her sleep, she heard a voice speaking to her. Suddenly, she woke up and looked out of the window and wondered whether she was over Jamaica and just about to land. Realising it was the man sitting next to her who spoke, she smiled at him.

He smiled at her and spoke again, "I'm sorry I woke you up, ma'am. I didn't realise you were sleeping."

"That's quite all right," Martha told him with an embarrassed look on her face. "I must have dozed off."

The stranger looked at her again.

"My name is Jacky Delaney. The scenery out there is so breathtaking, I couldn't help but want to share it with you. Just look at those grey and blue skies chasing each other. And the sun! You can't see it from here, but you know it's there because it glistens on the aeroplane's wing every few seconds."

Martha stared out of the window and nodded in agreement. Softly she told him, "Yes, it's beautiful isn't it?" She turned to face him. "I might as well introduce myself. My name is Martha Faraday."

"Might I call you Martha or Mrs Faraday?" asked the stranger.

Martha shrugged her shoulders. "Oh, either will do nicely, but you can call me Martha. Everybody does, including Connie and Pete."

He looked at her, somewhat puzzled. "Connie? Pete?"

Martha smiled at him. "They are the names of my two children. Connie is sitting on this very plane, away up front with her working partners. She's on a modelling assignment."

Jack listened attentively and appeared to be puzzled about her presence in a seat so far from her daughter.

"Your daughter's job sounds very nice, Martha, but why have you got to travel with her?"

Martha considered his inquisitive question. Smiling at him, she told him, "I'm going for a holiday. It was Connie's idea about me chaperoning her while holidaying. I haven't had one since I became a widow eight years ago. Jake made sure I kept my livelihood going in the little bakery he owned. He taught me everything about dough making." She threw her head back, stared at the roof of the plane and expressed how she felt about her little business. "It gives me great pleasure at Christmas and Easter to create novelty figures in the form of pastries for the children. You ought to see how their little faces light up." Suddenly she repositioned herself in her seat, stopped talking and apologised to him, "Pardon me for carrying on, Mr Delaney. All this talk about kneading dough and making snowmen must bore you terribly."

He smiled at her, amused. "Far from it, Martha, in fact, I find it quite interesting. It's a far cry from what I do for a living. That's what makes it so interesting. It's new to the ears. So don't think I'm bored by it. I tell you, there's nothing worse than talking shop with people in the same business as I am. It sends me off to sleep."

Martha thought he was very funny and laughed at his comments. As she laughed, she noted the outline of his face, his tall, lean figure, and his shoulder-length hair swept to one side of his forehead.

Forty-eight years that is more or less his age, thought Martha, *he is extremely handsome and debonair, despite his greying sideburns. I wonder what his motives for travelling to Jamaica are.*

As if he read her thoughts, he then told her, "I'm going to Jamaica on business. The company I work for asked me to go and look for a place, a nice location. I figure I'll be there for several weeks." He laughed, making it known he was not sorry either.

"Good for you!" replied a disenchanted Martha. "It sounds like an interesting place. I hope you find it."

Still looking pleased with himself, he replied, "It had better be just the type of place we're after or I won't have a job. The others will be following in a week's time."

Suddenly, the announcement came for them to fasten their seat belts for landing. Everyone got excited, peering out of windows over one another's heads and shoulders for a glimpse of Jamaica. No one was interested in a conversation at that time, but a safe landing into glorious sunshine.

As they left the plane, Jack Delaney gave Martha the option to go first.

"You have a wonderful holiday now," he told her, waving. "No doubt we shall see each other on a beach."

Martha smiled and waved, but said nothing, Meeting Jack Delaney was a good start to her holiday, but she was sorry their acquaintance had to end so soon.

Arriving at the hotel, she unpacked everything. Connie and her friend Debbie obliged by keeping out of the way. They manicured each other's fingernails and experimented with their hair. Martha thought she would give them the day off, rather than shout at them. Connie walked into the room a few minutes later.

"Have you by any chance unpacked my yellow shorts?" she asked. "I'm going to have a shower, and then I'll change into something comfortable. The sunshine is too glorious to ignore."

Martha looked at her alarmingly.

"Sunbathing so soon? Well, what about Miles and Roland? Won't they be joining us?"

"Yes certainly. They'll be joining us soon, but not for work, for tea and supper. Miles never works on the day he lands, even if it's early morning. He says he likes to get the feel of the place first, watch the natives, see the animals, and hear the local music. All these factors make him a better director behind the camera.

Martha sat mesmerised listening to Connie's description of Miles. Suddenly, as if in a trance, she got out of her seat and began walking around the room.

She whispered, "Yes, I can see what you mean. I can actually feel it myself." Gradually her pace got quicker, and with hands thrusting about she chanted, "Throw your head about like the natives, Connie. Yank your hips to the right like they do, Connie. Stroke your fingers through your hair, Connie. Let it stream backwards carelessly with the wind, Connie. And don't forget to smile, Connie, show your teeth while doing all that."

The sound of Debbie's footsteps approaching the room made her stop.

"Hey, Mother!" shouted Connie. "I didn't know you could act. That was brilliant."

Martha replied cheerfully, "That was no acting; that was mimicry. In other words, I was just trying to get into the holiday spirit. I hope Miles Daley doesn't hear of it."

Connie smiled lovingly at her. "I can see you intend to make the most of your three weeks in Jamaica. What about that nice man you were sitting with on the plane, the one you introduced to me when I passed to go to the powder room? Is he staying in these parts?

"Oh, you mean Mr Delaney. He was travelling alone but obviously married. I told him all about you, Pete, Jake and the bakery, but he said nothing about his social background. He told me he was here on business, looking over a place."

"What place?" Connie asked.

"I don't know. I think he was about to tell me when the plane landed. So did my thoughts, only mine was a crash landing. Why else would his leaving worry me? The only thing he said when we parted was he hoped we would meet on a beach, which is a million-to-one chance in a place like the island."

Miles Daley was all set for work the next day. He was up at 5 a.m. and made sure the hotel staff woke the others up in time for 6 a.m. breakfast.

"Breakfast at 6 a.m.!" screamed Martha. "I can't take it, I'll be sick."

"No, you won't!" shouted Miles. "In this part of the world, everything starts at 5 a.m., so by 6 a.m. you'll be starving. The heat takes a lot of your energy away, even when you're asleep! At 6 a.m. there'll be so much noise and commotion going on outside you won't be able to sleep anyway."

Every morning they sauntered down to the breakfast room with their luggage for the day's shooting, refreshments, water and fresh clothing. Everyone seemed well alert and rather used to that type of life, except Martha.

Miles took turns with Roland to drive the jeep over the rugged roads. Debbie and Connie posed for titillating pictures under waterfalls. Among sauntering giraffes, leaping antelopes and beautiful flamingos. It was obvious Connie and Debbie were enjoying every minute of their work and so were Miles and Roland. They got their satisfaction by taking out good shots, but at the moment, it was Martha and the photographers who were doing all the hard work. Martha carried the girls' suitcases, looked after their clothes, helped with their make-up and prepared refreshments. Roland and Miles had to move from one beauty spot to another with heavy equipment on their backs around their necks and under their arms.

Miles was in a good mood the first week. Apart from taking snaps, he went shopping with Martha and the girls for food. The only odd thing was that he always took a camera.

As they strolled through the native market one day, a little boy of about ten approached him, shouting, "You film man, bwana? You from Ol' Plantation Creek? Me very good helper if you take me with you."

Miles picked up a peculiar-looking fruit and weighed it in his hand. He looked menacingly at the boy.

"Me no from Ol' Plantation Creek, boy. Me no film man. Now shove off!"

The boy stood there, looking disappointed, with his head down.

The fruit seller butted in, "The boy is right, bwana. They're making film over at Ol' Plantation Creek. Very good film. Everybody go there looking for work."

Miles looked at him sheepishly. "How do you know?" he asked the fruit seller.

"Because they come twice a week in two jeeps to buy plenty food and fruits. Sometimes they bring big camera on sticks and film whole market, and anybody they film they give money."

Miles patted the boy on the head. "You know—"

"Me name Danni Rastar."

"Well, Danni Rastar, I'm not a film man, but perhaps you would like a little job taking some fruit back to our hotel?"

His eyes lit up with glee.

"Yes, bwana. This one very nice fruit. This one also, and that one very popular. People from film buy plenty of those."

The fruit seller confirmed Danni's statement and prepared a basket of fruit for Mile's approval.

Roland was less of an extrovert. He never spoke unless someone else spoke first. In the village square, the only things he was interested in were the ornaments and other artefacts the natives made. He bought pieces of all shapes and sizes to take home. Apart from that, he was well capable of helping and advising when Mile got stuck.

In the bar that night, Miles enquired about Ol' Plantation Creek.

The barman replied, "Ol' Plantation Creek? It's about twenty miles from here, sir. Everywhere you look it's breathtaking scenery. There is a mountain peak on one side, a waterfall on the other, and a camp near the centre. It's a park, with all kinds of animals, rivers, streams, beautiful gardens, and beautiful trees. You name it, it's there, sir."

"Sounds very grand," Miles said to him cheerfully. "I hear they are making a film there."

The barman nodded.

"Our work here is almost finished. Perhaps we'll take a ride over there tomorrow and have a look at them working."

The barman smiled and poured himself another drink.

"You can even finish taking pictures of models there," he said. "Very good pictures you'll get. Famous part of Jamaica."

The next day, as they trundled along twenty miles of rough road, through the jungle thicket, passing hungry wild animals, Martha got worried.

She fumed at Miles Daley, "I suppose you're enjoying all this? It was your idea for us to stray so far away from our base. Well! I'd rather be back in civilization. The sooner we leave for England the better."

Connie was getting worried about her mother's temper.

Worriedly, she told her, "Be brave and keep quiet. The wild animals won't get to us. All we're doing is changing our venue for a day to make our trip more interesting."

Miles could not help laughing. He giggled and chuckled at their conversation without commenting before adding, "I'm having a wonderful time. What about you, Roland?"

Sitting diagonally from Debbie, Roland was interested in her smile.

The film crew were pleased to see a party of English folks approaching and welcomed them in. Miles introduced himself as the lead photographer looking for a hot location.

"Well, you've come to the right place," the man replied in a broad Texan accent. "I'm the producer. My man Frank found us this beautiful place. Them folks back in Texas are gonna love this picture show."

Debbie whispered to Connie, "They are Americans, Connie. Now is our chance to show off our looks."

Martha overheard her. "Well, Connie, you might just be disappointed. I spoke to two on my way in and they weren't Americans. In fact, I recognised their accent and it was common Cockney."

Connie, being her usual confident self, replied, "Never mind the accent, Debbie. Mingling with the film set is what we want."

Although life was buzzing at Ol' Plantation Creek, something seemed wrong. People were moving about, putting up props, taking down props and standing about talking in groups, but the cameras were not rolling.

Martha and the girls wandered around, looking at everything. Miles strolled around, trying to look important with an oversized camera around his neck.

"What's the name of the film?" Miles asked a friendly-looking face. "If it ain't *The African Queen,* Bob's my uncle."

The man looked at him sideways and grinned. "I'm afraid Bob's your uncle because it ain't. It's called *The Lion Tamer."*

Miles returned his grin and remarked, "That's very appropriate, but why aren't the cameras rolling? Where is the star? Has he or she forgotten the lines?"

The man replied, "One of the supporting actresses has fallen ill. We can't work without her."

"We? Her?" asked Miles.

"Yes, me, I'm the director. She is supposed to be the star's mother-in-law. There are only four actresses on the set. The other three are very young. The make-up artist says he hasn't got the material to make a twenty-year-old girl look fifty, not here in the tropics in this heat. Her face would crack. I tell you she'll have to crawl on that set tomorrow. I shan't wait another day."

Miles stood up with elbows raised at his side. He looked as if he was part of the team.

"Aren't you being a little hard on the poor women?" he asked the director. "She's probably caught a fever."

The director raised his eyebrows in anger, but before he could speak the producer, Jack, walked towards them smiling. He patted the director on the shoulder.

"Richard Warburton, I've got some good news and some bad news for you."

Richard gave him a strained look.

"Well, let me have the bad news first."

"The bad news is Mrs Hamburg was seen by the doctor and he's ordered her to go into the hospital. He says her malaria is very bad."

Richard stared at him in disbelief.

"Well, if that's the bad news, Jack, there can't be any good news. This picture is finished. Do you think I can afford to pay a whole cast and feed ten hungry lions until Mrs Hamburg leaves the hospital?"

Jack Delaney backed away from him in fear.

"Well, I'm very optimistic that the good news might help. The rumour is that there is almost a lookalike of Mrs Hamburg walking around the film set at this very minute. Perhaps she could stand in for her."

"Have you seen her?" Richard asked quietly.

"No. They tell me she came in with the small party to look around."

Richard threw his hands up in the air and said, "Well, find her. Bring her to me now, before she leaves."

Just then Miles Daley butted in, "Just a minute. I came in with two young models and the mother of one of the girls. You don't mean Martha Faraday, do you? She's about forty-four, but she's no actress. The only acting she's capable of is acting the fool. She gave me a right ticketing off on the way here for driving through jungles and scaring her with wildcats."

Richard nodded his head and smiled optimistically. "That's the kind of star I like, one with a bit of punch. I hope she's a good lookalike."

Jack Delaney, looking more confident, told him, "I never realised it was Martha Faraday they were talking about. We sat next to each other on the plane from London. She was staying in a village some thirty miles from here."

Jack and Miles found Martha and the girls wandering around talking to film cameramen. Jack shouted her name. Martha turned around.

"Well, if it isn't Jack. Small island, isn't it? Is this place you came to look over, then?"

Jack replied, "Um, yes. They're making an American picture for worldwide distribution."

"But, Jack, you're British."

"I know I am, but this film is for international distribution and you're to star in it."

Martha held on to her bag and felt her chest to see if she was still breathing.

"First you woke me up on the plane, and now you're playing childish games with me."

Miles Daley interrupted, "It's no game, Martha, he means it. One of the characters, your lookalike, was admitted to hospital with malaria, which has left them in a spot."

Suddenly Connie intervened, "My mother knows nothing about acting. I suggest you use your understudy. Bringing my mother on this holiday has been a bad experience for her."

Richard Warburton, growing impatient, had tracked the others down. Scanning Martha from afar, he decided she was right for the part. "Your mother is not an actress?" he asked Connie. "Why don't you let her decide for herself? In some scenes, she'll appear in the background. Scenes with dialogue will take up only about thirty minutes, and that includes the other people's lines. I'm sure she can manage to learn her part by morning."

Martha nodded her head in approval and smiled surreptitiously, beaming with pride.

Connie was adamant and persistent with her protest, "But we have to get back to town before dark," she said. "It's all right for Mother, but what about me? I can't afford to get my skin blemished. There are too many mosquitoes out here. No wonder your lady has got malaria."

"Me too," added Debbie. "My skin has to be flawless."

"Don't worry about going back tonight," Miles reassured them. "Tomorrow at sunset will do nicely. In fact, I want to take some pictures of the girls in that lovely park near here, and I intend to pick up a few tips from the cameraman here. Who knows, I might even switch jobs when I get back to England."

Roland, who stood quietly taking it all in, laughed at Miles's comment, and taunted him, "When would you like me to start calling you Sir Miles?"

Martha got impatient and shouted at them, "You're all being very childish. Well, I'm staying. This is an opportunity I won't let slip. You can all return without me if you like. I'll make my own way back to England whenever."

With that, Richard Warburton giggled and ushered her along. "That's what I was waiting to hear Mrs Faraday, your decision. Now go with Jack Delaney and sign the necessary papers. After that, he'll take you to the make-up artist to prepare you for a screen test. When I've seen the screen test, I'll give you the script with your lines for you to learn tonight. Oh, and Jack Delaney will see that you all get looked after free of charge tonight."

With that, he walked away and left them to their fate.

Within two hours, Martha had undergone a quick transformation. The hairdresser and make-up artist had made a star of her.

It was very hard, if not totally impossible, to distinguish between her and the shots of Mrs Hamburgh in earlier scenes. Her silky, dark hair, her height and her figure – everything was perfect. Even the tone of her voice was exactly right.

Martha loved every minute of her star treatment and acted the part well. The character she played was a sophisticated, fastidious mother-in-law who interfered in everything her daughter- and son-in-law did.

Her son-in-law, the lion tamer, got his own back by using the lions to frighten her so he and his wife could have some privacy. Martha immersed herself in the part. Her character had a crisp walk, a posh accent and a nose for picking up hints, not forgetting a tongue to make people cry.

The only thing that worried her was that she could see Connie was jealous. Connie was the one with the youthful looks, the gorgeous figure, the beautiful mermaid-like hair. *Why didn't she get a part?* Martha asked herself. Still, Connie was her only beloved daughter. They must never quarrel.

Placing Connie on her knee an hour before filming was due to start, she told her, "Don't be hard on me getting this part, Connie. It just happens that they want an older person. You've brought me on a holiday of a lifetime, and a holiday of a lifetime it has been. That I'm grateful for. You're still young and beautiful and I'm sure someday you'll accomplish your dream of a lifetime."

Connie hugged her mother and kissed her on the forehead. "I apologise for not encouraging you, Mother," she said. "As you say, I'm still young with endless opportunities ahead."

No sooner had Connie got off Martha's knee than Jack Delaney came over and told Connie that Richard Warburton had suggested she and Debbie fall into one of the scenes as extras. No signatures were needed for their parts, but he suggested they leave their names and addresses for future reference. Connie could not believe her ears.

Martha winked at Connie and whispered, "See what I told you?"

Miles and Roland had their dream of a lifetime helping with the film cameras and had their names entered in the credits.

As they collected their payment and drove out of Plantation Creek, they were stopped by a small boy begging for a lift. Miles braked sharply and reversed back in a hurry.

Peering at the boy, he shouted, "My, if it ain't Danni Rastar!"

There was silence, then a peering session, and then everyone shouted simultaneously, "It is Danni Rastar!"

"What brought you so far from home? Is there no school today?" Miles asked.

The boy gave him a manly reply, "Danni Rastar come here to look for work. Danni oldest of seven children. Me work some days, go school some days. Danni need lift from bwana to go home with parcel."

"Jump in," Miles told him with a broad grin on his face. "Sit next to anyone you fancy."

"Sweet child," Martha declared, peering down at him.

"He can sit next to me anytime."

"And did you find work, Danni Rastar?" Miles giggled.

"No, bwana. Work no find, but film people give me clothes, shoes, money and food. All sorts to take home for everyone in family. Bwana say he was no film man back at market the day me Bwoy take fruit basket to hotel, but bwana did come to ol' Jamaica Creek. Very funny."

"We came looking for work too, Danni, and we came to see film man make picture. That's why we came to ol' Jamaica Creek."

The boy gave an angelic grin, nodded his head as the jeep rocked from side to side and replied, "Bwana, like Danni, no luck with work."

With that, he shut up for the remaining journey except for pointing out strange animals and saying thanks when Miles dropped him off.

Three days later, as they boarded the plane for home, Martha looked back at Jamaica and said to Connie, "Pete and Walter will need a lot of convincing when we tell them everything that has happened."

The Enlightenment Summary

Martha Faraday was the proud owner of a little bakery her husband, Jake, had left her. She served her village well but longed for a life of ease and pleasure. Her wish was granted when her only daughter, Connie, who was a model, invited her to travel on an assignment to Jamaica. On the aeroplane, Martha had the misfortune of sitting on her own, away from Connie and her work party. She was lucky to sit next to a fine man, who spoke to her.

The holiday in Jamaica was very trying. Martha not only had to carry their luggage over the rough terrain but had to wash their clothes and cook as well.

In the village, while shopping for food, they came across a young boy who told them about a location some miles away where filming was going on. Shortly afterwards, they were heading for Rhino Creek, the location. Miles, the lead photographer.

About the Author

Deeta was born in the 1940s in a beautiful country hamlet called Norwood, located in the parish of St. Ann, Jamaica.

Norwood is lush and green, with few houses, one or two shops, a Sunday school, and hardly anything else—except small landholdings and inhabitants who either know each other or are related.

Deeta's mother was a local self-taught midwife, and her father was a farmer and landowner. Deeta attended school in Ocho Rios, a tourist resort with Spanish-influenced naming traditions. The area is known for its rivers, such as Dunn's River, Big River, White River, and Milford River.

Deeta is one of six siblings.